GOLDEN

Rajasthan

GOLDEN

Rajasthan

KISHORE SINGH

Prakash Books

Publisher: Ashwani Sabharwal
Text: Kishore Singh
Editor: Monisha Mukundan
Design: Yogesh Suraksha Design Studio
www.ysdesignstudio.com

Published by
Prakash Book Depot
M-86 Connaught Circus.
New Delhi – 110 001. India.
Phone: 91-11-23416566/23416897
Fax: 23246975
Email : sales@prakashbooks.com
Website : www.prakashbooks.com

Printed and bound in India By
Brijbasi Art Press Ltd., New Delhi.

© Prakash Book Depot,2004

ISBN : 81-7234-060-5

contents

The Romance

OF RAJASTHAN

Life in the desert can be raw, leading to an inter-dependability on all available natural resources, including camels (facing page), goats (above) and cattle.
Preceding page: The 'ship of the desert' is perfectly adapted to walking on the soft sand
Page 6-7: The interiors of an apartment in Jodhpur's Mehrangarh Fort
Page 4-5: A lake-facing view of Udaipur's City Palace complex
Page 3-4: Women gathered together to celebrate the marital festival of Gangaur.

TODAY, THE DESERT SEEMS ROMANTIC, its men and women the inheritors of a gloriously chivalrous past, its arts an expression of a brave but sensitive race, its architecture the embodiment of strength and grace. These clichés contain, as clichés often do, a kernel of truth and yet they obscure the very real heroism and tenacity of a people who tamed their hostile environment, creating beauty from the rock and sand of barren lands and developing a code of living that was as implacable as the desert in which they lived.

The earliest inhabitants of this part of western India were tribes who settled in a few fertile tracts, and groups of nomads who travelled with their herds from one oasis to another. The first chieftains who carved themselves tenuous fiefdoms out of this inhospitable landscape were probably more foolhardy than brave. And yet they remained, sustaining their hegemony over their lands through stern vigilance and military strength. Gradually, these early fiefdoms developed into flourishing kingdoms. The rulers fought each other constantly, so that each one developed a warlike ethos and a defensive style of architecture. Trade sustained them, for the trade route into the fabulously rich plains of India lay through their lands.

Collectively, these princely states came to be known as Rajputana, the abode of princes, and today we know it as the modern India state of Rajasthan. It was not entirely desert. There were hills here, green sanctuaries where tigers roamed, and herds of deer provided ample sport to people raised on the might of arms. There were lakes, hidden like jewels amidst the rocky escarpments of a wind-ravaged terrain. As war gave way to diplomacy and times of peace, the princes of Rajasthan ventured forth from the fastnesses of their forbidding forts, to build lavishly-appointed hunting lodges and delicately wrought summer palaces besides their lakes. As trade burgeoned and traders prospered, cities rose out of the sand, decorated with all the skill of a rich inheritance of craftsmanship and all the decorative influences of a widening horizon of activity nurtured by contact with the other states of India and with the world.

Steadfastness, loyalty, unflinching courage were valued by the people of Rajasthan. Unswerving devotion to deities and to leaders was a base upon

which their society was built. The Rajputs never went to war without paying homage to their *kul-devis* and *devatas*, the family deities. And the living examples of these deities, the contemporary saints and seers, made a deep impression upon their minds. War was a part of the ethos. When the fortunes of war turned, the practice of *jauhar*, the mass self-immolation by women, and the men's suicidal defence of beleaguered forts gave the Rajputs an aura of mystic courage and self-sacrifice that time has not dulled.

And yet, in a brutal, war-torn past, history is full of examples of Rajput sensitivity. Meera Bai, the legendary poet-princess, left her royal home and husband because she wanted to worship Krishna. She is credited with writing some fine verses and *Krishna-bhajans*, many of which are still sung today. She travelled from place to place singing songs of love for Krishna, and died at a temple, virtually unrecognised. The beautiful Queen Padmini of Chittaurgarh is said to have won the heart of an invader, Allaudin Khilji, when he glimpsed her in a mirror. He resolved to win her hand, through battle if necessary and laid seige to the fort. He won the fort but he lost the queen to *jauhar*. And who can forget the romantic Prithviraj Chauhan, who spirited his beloved Sanjukta away from her father's court, where the bravest princes of the land had gathered in the hope of winning her hand. And certainly few royal families in the world can have suffered the deprivations that Rana Sangha and his family endured when he renounced the throne of Mewar and went into hiding in order to build up a force to challenge the might of Mughal power.

A period of peace and a series of political treaties in the nineteenth century, with the British rulers of India, brought Rajasthan into the modern world. Martial education gave way to the three Rs; and as royal schools were founded for the princes (where they enrolled and were accompanied by whole retinues of staff to cater to their personal needs), schools and colleges were also established for women. *Purdah*, the practice of veiling and secluding women, was dying a slow, natural death. However, even as the first decade of the twenty-first century is upon us, the *purdah* system continues to exist in Rajasthan.

In times of peace, the princes cultivated two pastimes: polo and *shikar*. The game of polo had its origins in India, but it was the British who took up the game, gave it rules; and with the adoption of the famous Jodhpuri breeches and riding boots, the sport moved to an international arena. The Rajasthani royals practised it with a skill and dexterity that remained unchallenged for decades. They had well-stocked stables, and talk of polo was as frequent as that of the weather.

Shikar was a winter event in Rajasthan. Shooting tiger, bagging wild boar and deer, arranging the best wild grouse shoots: the maharajas were adept at the sport, and often used hunting as a means of inviting the British viceroy to their kingdoms, establishing social channels of communication in order to gain political or economic ends. It is said that the project that created the Gang Canal to carry water to the thirsty desert was negotiated by Bikaner's Maharaja Ganga Singh purely by such diplomacy. Today, with

Men wear huge turbans (top), and women in long skirts and mantles walk for miles with pitchers on their heads in search of water (above), saturating the desert with their bright, jewel-like colours. The architecture of the desert cities is no less impressive, and brings distinction to the landscape, as in the case of the tiered Hawa Mahal (facing page) that forms one part of the façade of Jaipur's formally designed City Palace.

shikar banned, and wildlife running low, the former royals have turned their attention to an affiliated field: conservation.

The nineteenth and twentieth century maharajas adapted to Western ways, were known by Western pet-names, and in society columns were frequently referred to as the Jaipurs or the Bundis or the Jodhpurs. When they travelled to England, the maharanis shed the confines of the *purdah* system and dressed in slacks. The wealth and lavish lifestyles of the royal families created an aura of glamour and tales of extravagant eccentricities began to circulate in fashionable London. There came a time when prominent jewellers in the West started fashioning Indian jewellery for the princes were major buyers of such 'trinkets'.

When the railways first came to India, the princes were among the first to develop their state railways. A number of the trains that run even today ply on tracks laid by the princes of these states. Travellers can sample some of the excitement of early train travel in the comfort of the Palace on Wheels train that does a tourist circuit in the winter season. The original carriages once belonged to the royal homes of Rajasthan, but even the new are luxuriously furnished: living rooms, dining rooms, kitchens, bars and bedrooms, each fitted out in sumptuous splendour. Much of Rajasthan's past now lies in museums, in palace hotels, and in its continuing traditions of fine craftsmanship. When India won its independence from the British, the

The Palace on Wheels train offers a royal experience (below). Preceding Pages: For men and women, the annual camel fair at Pushkar, held in November, is an occasion to strike business deals, renew contacts, and bargain for household implements. While trading for camels and horses remains its main focus, it also has a spiritual dimension as people gather to pray at Brahma's temple and bathe in the holy pond called Sarovar.

royal kingdoms merged with the Indian republic and became part of the union. The maharajas were given important government posts, often-diplomatic assignments. Privy purses allowed them to maintain the privileged lifestyles to which they were accustomed. Then, the privy purses were withdrawn, and a limit placed on the amount of property, wealth and land an individual could possess. This led to hasty sales and certain dowdiness in the maintenance of royal buildings. Tourism has provided new life-blood. Palaces are now hotels and for a price, visitors may have the pleasure of not only staying in palaces, but also meeting the former maharajas and their families. Family heirlooms and wealth have found their way into public museums: open to view and display, never to be the private property of individual families again. Rumours abound of gold and jewels hidden in fort and palace walls, but no one knows if any of these have any basis in fact.

Fortunately, the palace hotels and museums and the growing interest in the state's princely past has ensured markets for Rajasthani craftsmanship and the survival of Rajasthan's heritage. Good sense and aesthetic value continue to characterise daily life in the desert. It has been so for hundreds of years.

An age has come to pass; the cities flourish; during festivals, there is still an explosion of colour. The Rajputana has discovered gold in its sands. Rajasthan is golden, a royal symbol of India.

The terrain may be sandy for most part, but Rajasthan's Aravalli hills are also the perfect place for providing shelter to a variety of wildlife. This includes the tiger that can be spotted at two of its natural parks – Sariska and Ranthambhor (below). Such parks were created by the erstwhile maharajas as shooting reserves, but have since been used for the conservation of wildlife as well as avifauna.

The women of Rajasthan are resplendent in their clothes and jewellery. For those who belong to the state, it is easy enough to tell the community or tribe of each person based on their vestments and accessories.
Women wear both gold and silver, and some continue to veil their face in public, or before their elders (facing page). The Sapera or snake-dancer community is invited at large fairs to perform before an audience (above), though only a few decades ago they had almost lost their skills for lack of patronage.

Men are no less distinctive in their raiment, and often flaunt as much jewellery as the women (facing page). This is particularly so in rural pockets where the measure of a man is still his traditional garb. In the cities, such as this street in Jaipur (above), even though they may have become more urbanised, the men still sport a distinctive look characteristic of the people of Rajasthan, making it perhaps the only state with an unbroken, cultural lineage.

DANGER
खतरनाक
क्षेत्र
रास्ता बन्द है

RAJASTHAN GOVERNMENT
ARCHAEOLOGY & MUSEUMS DEPT T.
VISIT PATWA HAVELI
ENTRANCE FEE 2

FORTS
and Palaces

Patwon-ki-Haveli in Jaisalmer (facing page) and the victory tower at Chittaurgarh (above). The masons and architects worked closely to create a language that used stone as a flexible, even malleable, material for building the desert's fabulous buildings. Stone was pierced, crenellated, sculptured and surmounted with pillars, arches, balconies, domes, eaves and cusped windows that transformed the whole effect into delicate filigree.

MILITARY STRATEGY DICTATED THAT FORTIFICATIONS be raised on an elevated spot, and Chittaurgarh, Kumbhalgarh, Meherangarh and Nahargarh are among examples of the most extensive forts ever built in this country. Others like Kota and Bikaner did not have the advantage of height, so moats were created here to encircle the fortifications. Jaisalmer's battlements rise like sheer cliffs from a flat sea of sand, making it practically unassailable. In times of peace, the maharajas built delicate palaces, incorporating the best from Rajput, Mughal and British architecture. These buildings are either splendidly handsome, as Umaid Bhawan Palace in Jodhpur is, or exquisitely pretty, such as the Lake Palace in Udaipur.

Rarely has the world seen such thoughtful divisions of space as exists in Jaipur's City Palace, with units that were integrated within the design of the entire city, the whole being conceived of as a single entity. Bundi's palaces are intricately overlaid with fine murals. Bikaner's Lallgarh Palace suggests both strength and delicacy, most accurately symbolising the Rajput temperament.

The palaces had to suit the dual lifestyle of the royals: they had to function as modern residences, as well as traditional Indian style palaces in which it was essential that there be separate women's quarters and corridors through which women could move from one area to another in privacy. Though the maharajas also built separate summer residences, the main palace almost inevitably had a room designed so that breeze flowed freely through it, where the royals could relax on a hot summer afternoon in the comfort of perfumed, cooling breezes.

While later palaces had grand, sweeping staircase in the best Continental tradition, and were surrounded by open gardens, many of the earlier palaces were built within fortified walls and characterised by narrow staircases and unimpressive entrances to the royal apartments. These had a purpose: in case of invasion, even a single warrior could defend the entry to the private apartments while the royals escaped through secret corridors!

The maharajas were quick to accept the latest innovations from the West and these were introduced into their newer palaces. They were illuminated with electricity soon after it was introduced to India. Formal landscaped gardens were carefully tended. There were smoking rooms and morning rooms in the British tradition, several guest rooms, and suites for the maharaja and the maharani. Often there were two separate dining halls, one in the Indian style, the other Western. Airconditioning in its basic form, and electric lifts were first used at Jodhpur's Umaid Bhawan Palace in the early years of the last century.

A large number of luxurious palaces were built in the nineteenth and early twentieth century for a variety of reasons. Jaipur had its City Palace and other royal buildings, because the ruler wanted to shift his capital from Amber where there was no room to expand, to a new capital city. Jodhpur's Umaid Bhawan Palace was built to provide employment during a terrible famine. Lallgarh Palace was commissioned because Maharaja Ganga Singh required a modern residence.

It was not just the architecture of the palaces that was spectacular; their furnishing also set them apart from other grand residences. Elaborate architectural motifs were picked out in window screens, pavilions, balconies, cupolas and turrets. Inside the palaces, French tapestry, French and English furniture, Belgian suites and Bohemian crystal chandeliers were used to create the world's richest homes. The look could be formal, or art deco. Often, sadly, it was eccentric because the royals shopped indiscriminately and shipped back everything that caught their fancy in Europe and England. Faberge eggs sat beside onyx lamps, and the Swiss watch industry worked

As architecture evolved, and the threat of frequent battles receded, architects spent a greater part of their time and attention focusing on the interiors of palaces. The 'sheesh mahal', adopted in many of the palaces, used bits of mirrors set within gilded forms (below), and was adapted from Mughal palaces. Mostly, though, interiors were profusely painted (facing page), covering from walls and ceilings to pillars and arches, to create pleasure pavilions for the princes and the nobility.

overtime to keep royal households supplied with a clock for each mantel-piece, and there were often more than a hundred! Carpets worth small fortunes were casually flung in the halls, on staircases, and in cars. Silver and gold appointments in certain palace suites were common. In the ballroom, wood floors were provided for Western ballroom dancing. Those halls in which traditional *mujras* were staged were heavily carpeted. Inevitably too, trophies of hunts graced dining rooms and billiards rooms, and the maharaja's study.

During the Mughal period, Rajasthan's maharajas favoured *pietra dura* inlay work. Durbar Halls were adorned with gold and precious stonework on marble. A particularly popular element in palaces of that period were rooms in which mirror mosaic brought sparkle and colour into a room: these *sheesh mahals* or halls or mirrors may be seen in almost every palace built during the Mughal period. While the maharajas were building palaces, the Rajasthani nobles built small *havelis* or mansions structured around a courtyard or a series of courtyards, with a *zenana* for the women, and a segregated front area strictly for male visitors. While beautiful *havelis* came up in almost every major Rajasthani principality, the most outstanding examples are the *havelis* of Jaisalmer with their breathtakingly lovely facades of pierced stone screens.

Rajasthan's merchant class was originally from the Shekhawati region, and this trading community gave the state yet another kind of *haveli*, not architecturally noteworthy, but magnificently decorated with murals. Almost every available surface of the walls was covered with paintings, depicting religious and social themes. The dry desert climate of the area has ensured the survival of these paintings and they remain in a remarkably good state of preservation. An interesting facet of these frescoed *havelis* was that over the years the artists became more ambitious in their range of subjects; having heard of *memsahibs* who drove cars, of steam engines and trains that carried large numbers of travellers, of the fashionable dress of the Raj, but without having seen any of these wonders for themselves, they painted these subjects as they were described to them or as they had been depicted in pictures that came their way. The results are sometimes hilarious, but almost always imaginative and original. Occasionally religious themes got mixed with the social, and the result was paintings such as the one depicting the monkey god, Hanuman driving a Rolls Royce with Lord Ram, accompanied by Sita, in the back seat!

Rajasthan's architectural mix was fairly eclectic, and often depended on the whims of the maharajas. Some palaces are examples of pure Rajput architecture; while others have incorporated a bit of British suburbia into the deserts of Rajasthan. There was a casual breeziness about the opulence of the palaces. And yet, the maharajas knew their architectural wealth could invite envy and even lead to war. It is said that before Jaipur was founded, Emperor Akbar made a pilgrimage to Ajmer in Rajasthan; Sawai Jai Singh of Amber, fearing the emperor's envy and acquisitiveness, failed to invite him to Amber, with its beautiful courtyards and sumptuously decorated rooms.

An attendant at Amber Fort, Jaipur in full ceremonial dress (above), and exterior views of Meherangarh Fort, Jodhpur and Junagarh Fort, Bikaner (facing page). The tectonic seats of the heads of the clans were bequeathed to the maharajas as part of the settlement when they merged with India, and mostly trusts and foundations are responsible for their upkeep and maintenance. Clan memorabilia is displayed inside, in museums especially created for the purpose.
Preceding pages: The rounded bastions of Jaisalmer Fort, and the magnificent Umaid Bhawan Palace, Jodhpur. Twenty-two princely kingdoms once made up the state of Rajasthan.

Of all the cities, Jaipur is Rajasthan's youngest, designed in the early eighteenth century by Sawai Jai Singh II, who moved his capital from nearby Amber (facing page). At the heart of the new city is the City Palace (above) where Rajput elements have been combined with the Mughal to create a complex which is as detailed on the outside as within the grand suites of its apartments.

Though his architect, Vidyadhar, gave the palace a distinctive look, he planned the city along a symmetrical grid that has survived into the twenty-first century.

And later, when he was aksed by the emperor to describe Amber, the maharaja sliced open a pomegranate and said, "Sire, this is Amber; tier upon tier of beautiful buildings!"

The state of Alwar remained insecure in its fortunes until its alliance with the British gave it a period of stability. There followed a period of intensive building activity. The first major residence in Alwar was Vinay Vilas, the city palace complex, built in the middle of the nineteenth century. The style was flamboyantly Rajput, with elements of Mughal influence and the addition of Western detail as well.

Much of the wealth of Alwar is still on display at the museum in the city palace, and from a window in the museum one can glimpse the exquisite Moosi Maharani Chhatri, built to commemorate the sati of Maharaja Bakhtawar Singh's mistress. It consists of a large cenotaph beside a water tank surrounded by temples. The entire complex is cradled in the hills that form a part of the natural defence of Alwar. In the distance stands Bala Qila, the original fort. Its typically Rajput architecture is evident both in the three-kilometre-long fortifications and in the residential apartments, which have some fine examples of gold leaf painting.

Alwar's other two palaces were built by Maharaja Jey Singh. He commissioned the delightful Italianate palace, Yeshwant Niwas, but soon after it was ready, he decided that he did not like his new palace and so a newer palace was begun, beside Vijay Sagar Lake, rising like an Oriental city from the banks of the lake, completed in 1927 and containing a magnificent 105 rooms.

The Lake Palace in Udaipur (below and facing page) has now been converted into a hotel, that has considerably altered its original, airier architectural design, while retaining most of its grandeur. It would be difficult to find a more romantic palace hotel in any other part of the world.

Bharatpur and Deeg, not far from Alwar, are impressive examples of Jat architecure. The impregnable fort at Bharatpur withstood a seige by the British in the early nineteenth century. Thereafter, the house of Bharatpur signed a peace treaty with the British and remained a powerful ally to the central power in Delhi.

Bharatpur Fort is an austere structure, without the ornamentation usually associated with buildings in Rajasthan. It was added to by succeeding generations of maharajas. Mahal Khas in the fort is an elegant example of palace architecture with its windows of stone lattice-work screens set in long, arched alcoves. The prominent Jat domed roof is in evidence here, and the walls are decorated with paintings. There are luxurious *hamams* or sunken baths with hot and cold water.

Lohagarh fort, also in Bharatpur, has two commemorative towers Jawahar Burj and Fateh Burj. Of these, Jawahar Burj is particularly noteworthy for there is an iron pillar here which acts as a family tree for the royal house of Bharatpur, recording in detail the names of all the rulers, beginning with Lord Krishna!

A degree of Western influence came to Bharatpur in the early twentieth century when Golbagh Palace was commissioned, complete with art nouveau pierced stone windows in a wing reserved exclusively for the ruler's daughters. Elaborate stonework characterised the palace, which combined elements of traditional Jat architecture with the fashionable Indo-Saracenic, and incorporated formal Mughal style gardens. Bharatpur was wildlife country, known for its tiger shoots, and at one stage the carpet

Following pages: The Lake Palace, formerly known as Jag Mandir, appears to float on the waters of the Pichola. Built by the rulers of Udaipur as a retreat from the summer heat, it can be reached only by boat. Later, another island palace, Jag Mandir, was built on the lake to house Shah Jahan as an honoured guest before he inherited the Mughal empire.

in Golbagh's library was made of tiger skins, and the chairs in the dining hall covered with deer hide. The Western style rooms of the palace were copied by the craftspeople from pictures in English magazines. The exterior of Golbagh, however, clearly belonged to the soil, with its brackets and balconies, its cupolas and staircases ornamented with stone screens.

Golbagh was an adaptation of the palaces in the earlier Jat capital of Deeg, a small distance away. Deeg is a veritable museum of Jat architecture for the complex remains untouched by time. The dominant domed roofs are in evidence here, and royal apartments located beside a small artificial lake have delightful decorative details. One of the quaintest parts of the palace is the sit-down dining area intended for traditional Indian meals, consisting of a U-shaped marble platform at which guests, seated cross-legged on brocade cushions on the floor, were served in traditional silver platters called *thalis*.

Among the palaces at Deeg are two pavilions called Sawan and Bhadon, built to resemble a pleasure barge. These airy apartments once had many devices which simulated rainfall, complete with falling water, and the sound of thunder. The pavilions formed part of the complex's Keshav Bhawan where five hundred fountains once spouted coloured water. There is also the eighteenth century Gopal Bhawan, where many rooms still have their original furniture, for the royal family was in residence here till three decades ago. Probably the most opulent building in Deeg is Suraj Bhawan, built of white marble, unlike the cream-coloured sandstones used for the other buildings, and inlaid with semi-precious stones.

Bikaner's Junagarh Fort is five centuries old, as ancient as the city, which was founded by Rao Bika, a scion of the house of Jodhpur. Today Bikaner is a flourishing city, and has some beautiful *havelis* made of carved sandstone, but since these are accessible only through narrow, crowded alleyways in the old city, they are still to be discovered by visitors. That discovery may take a few years, however, for the architecture in the rest of Bikaner is quite stunning, and few visitors venture beyond the main streets.

The ramparts of the Junagarh let form the fulcrum for the city of Bikaner. A moat surrounds the battlements. The palm prints of women who committed *sati* can still be seen beside the gates, grim reminders of the past. The first impression of the interior of Junagarh Fort is one of relative modernity, and with good reason, for here the apartments have been added to by succeeding generations of maharajas, and the latest additions are barely a century old. There are large open courtyards where public *durbars* were held, and shows staged. The maharajas sat under a marble canopy on a small artificial island built in a body of water, in cool and isolated splendour during such events.

Narrow staircases ensure privacy and security to residential apartments on a higher floor. In some rooms are ceramic Delft tiles, plastered upside down, for the masons, and possibly the occupants of the apartments, did not know any better. Screened corridors run the length of the apartments and they are beautifully lighted by small windows that are bejewelled with coloured glass.

There is Badal Mahal, the Hall of Clouds, painted with recurring images of rain-bearing clouds. In this hall is a portrait of Maharaja Sardar Singh painted by a Turkish artist. In common with most Rajasthani palaces, there is the inevitable but sumptuous *sheesh mahal*, a chamber decorated with thousands of tiny mirrors. The *piece de resistance* of Junagarh is Anup Mahal, the throne room, which appears to be lavishly embellished with gold leaf, and inlaid with a mosaic of precious and semi-precious stones. At closer examination it soon becomes evident that there is, in fact, no inlay, no gold. The maharaja of Bikaner, who was a regular visitor to the Mughal court in Delhi, wished to outdo the extravagant decorations in the halls of public and private audience at Delhi's Red Fort. But years of warfare had depleted the Bikaner treasury. The maharaja therefore, commissioned local workmen to simulate the rooms in Delhi. These skilled craftspeople created an illusion of marble walls using alabaster; the inlay and gold leaf are no more than finely executed paintings in the style that later came to be known as 'trompe l' oeil'.

With the British as allies, latter day pomp and ceremony required a court of quite another kind. This in Junagarh was the Durbar Hall, a formal room with teak panelled walls, a very high roof, columns, balconies, and a carpet that was woven within the room itself. Bikaner became famous for its carpets, and the palaces are furnished by some of the finest examples of this craft.

Lallgarh looks as if it were designed by a local architect. It is a perfect example of Rajput architecture, a huge building of red sandstone with a look of extreme fragility provided by its pierced stone window screens. As a matter of fact, the architect was an Englishman, Sir Swinton Jacob. Built on Rajput principles, around two courtyards, Lallgarh is a regal palace, with elaborate, formal entrances and encircling verandahs which insulate the rooms from the harsh desert sun. Cupolas decorate the façade, and the whole palace is a marvel of stone craftsmanship. The apartments within the palace are Western in style, and contain palatial rooms connected to one another by a network of corridors. There are halls in which to entertain guests, dining halls and separate residential wings for the royal princes. Stables and garages flank the extensive gardens. Lallgarh's expansive architecture and its extensive grounds are typical of later Rajasthani palaces, which were built in times of peace and required no protective fortifications. This turn-of-the century palace, along with Jodhpur's Umaid Bhawan Palace, is one of the most modern royal residences in the state.

Bundi was geographically isolated from the other Rajput states and the imperial rulers at New Delhi. As a result, its architecture was not influenced by other palaces in Rajasthan, nor by Mughal or British architecture. The largest of the palaces is the seventeenth century Chatar Mahal, located along the slope of a hill. Green-tinged serpentine plex, and the design is vintage Rajput with drooping, arcuate roofs. Serpentine is a hard stone unlike the sandstone used in other Rajput palaces, and so the surface is unadorned. Where there is decorative embellishment, it almost always features traditional motifs such as the elephant and the lotus.

In the eighteenth century, Bundi made one concession to the trends of the time, and some of the palace walls were painted in what was to become known as the Bundi style of painting. The *chitra shala* in Bundi has some of the best examples of this school of painting.

In the twentieth century, Maharaja Bahadur Singh succumbed to the need for a modern residence. This took the shape of a palace built beside an earlier hunting lodge. Phoolsagar, Bundi's twentieth century accoutrements of a modern palace; a ballroom, lavish guest apartments, and in the spirit of the area, shooting facilities. Work on the palace began in 1945; India gained independence in 1947; the states merged with the Indian union, and consequently, though it is a marvellous building, Phoolsagar remains incomplete.

Kota, which adjoins Bundi, was once part of this state and the two share a common history and artistic heritage. Its city palace rose over decades of intermittent warfare. High walls and strong, defensive ramparts enclose palaces of delicate stonework, fluted domes and elephant-shaped brackets. Art historian Percy Brown noted 'few signs of any ordered plan'. The walls were once inlaid with glass, ebony and ivory and remains of this may still be seen. The rooms are delightfully full of niches, alcoves, carvings and miniatures. There is a sense of excitement in Kota's architecture, particularly in its interiors. Since the City Palace was also the seat of power, it housed the court, the treasury, the garrison, the arsenal, ateliers, kitchens, stables, stores, and the homes of the palace staff. Parades used to be held, and processions assembled in Jalebi Chowk; Hathia Pol with its large image of an elephant is a typical Hadoti entrance gate. The kings of Kota held *durbar* in the Raj Bhavan which is decorated with friezes made of mirrors and paintings depicting the Krishnaleela. Halls of private audience, residential areas for the maharaja and the Zenana Mahal for the royal women are among the other buildings that are arranged in an informal pattern within the ramparts. In 1905, a second royal residence, Umed Bhawan, was designed by Sir Swinton Jacob, the architect who was responsible for Bikaner's Lallgarh. This Western style palace incorporates a banquet hall and as many as eight guest suites. Clearly, it was meant to be a place for leisure, and for entertaining state visitors.

The romance of Rajasthan's architecture is most clearly discernible in Jaipur. The city itself was established over two-and-a-half centuries ago, but the original capital of this state may be seen at Amber, the hill fort containing places from where the Kachchawaha clan ruled for centuries. Amber is guarded by two imposing forts on adjacent hilltops. Nahargarh Fort named after a tribal '*bhomia*' who resided there, was commissioned in 1734. A highlight of the fort is its complex, scientifically laid network of canals that collected and carried rainwater to large water tanks at Nahargarh and Jaigarh, the other forts close to Amber.

Jaigarh fort contains some very fine palaces, amongst them Laxmi Vilas which contains such luxuries as central heating and steam baths. Amber's maharajas continued to add to and alter its apartments, and in the early

A distinctive feature of the City Palace in Udaipur (above and facing page) is the quality of glass mosaic, an art that was learned from the ateliers of Italian craftsmen. It was soon given a Rajput sensibility, and lavishly used to decorate courtyards used for the entertainment of the maharanas of Mewar. Today, a scion of the house of Udaipur continues to inhabit one of the palaces within the complex, while the rest are open to guests as hotels, or museums.

eighteenth century it was given a comprehensive facelift by Vidyadhar, the architect who designed Rajasthan's first planned city, Jaipur.

Amber contains fairytale palaces set around courtyards, gardens and terraces, temples and public areas, each with architectural and decorative details that set them apart from any other palace. Some of the decorations, such as those at the Diwani-i-Am, the Hall of Public Audience, were so gorgeous, the ruler had them covered with stucco lest the Mughal emperor in Delhi be tempted to raid Amber. There are elaborate gates, dazzling entrances to palace apartments, such as the mosaic style Ganesh Pol. The square ivory panels at the Jai Mandir, the luxurious may still be seen, although the sumptuous furnishings and rich carpets are no longer there. Later, Jaipur established a peaceful relationship with the Mughals, and a daughter of the house of Amber married Emperor Akbar. The period of security that followed allowed the royal family to devote themselves to pursuits of leisure, and so they began to feel the need for a larger, less confined capital than fortified Amber. Sawai Jai Singh II took a keen interest in astronomy, architecture, town planning, music and art. He sought out skilled scholars who shared his interests and the most celebrated of these was Vidyadhar, an inspired architect, mathematician and town planner. Jaipur was elaborately planned on paper, on a grid pattern with straight interesting roads and residential areas clearly separated from commercial and trading zones. Shops of a uniform size were placed on wide avenues. Gardens were developed. Areas were set aside for different guilds of craftsmen, traders, professionals and for nobles. Individual plans for houses had to blend with the overall aesthetic planning of the city, and each plan had to be approved by Vidhyadhar himself. A beautiful city was in the making as early as 1728.

Royal Jaipur was a beautiful blend of Rajput and Mughal architecture. Decorative motifs such as pillars, arches and windows were predominantly Mughal. Also Mughal in style was the placement of buildings for different functions in separate areas, surrounded by their own independent gardens. The progression of the buildings was dictated by the royal lifestyle, so that the stables gave way to administrative offices, guest apartments, the hall of public audience and then the hall of private audience, the treasury, the subsidiary royal places, and in the centre of the entire complex, like a jewel within a beautiful box were the royal apartments. The royal residence, Chandra Mahal, was the pivot around which the new city was built. This pyramidal seven-storey palace is distinctly Rajput in style. Within the palace complex is also housed the temple of Govind Dev; and as many as thirty-six ateliers and fifty-two administrative departments. Perhaps the most amazing structure in Jaipur is the dramatically beautiful Jantar Mantar, an observatory of enormous stone instruments created by the astronomer king to maintain Jaipur time, to read altitudes and azimuths and to calculate celestial latitudes and longitudes.

No account of Jaipur would be complete without reference to the palaces beyond the city palace complex. Rambagh Palace was initially a hunting lodge that was turned into a princely retreat with the addition of pavilions and gardens. Still later, such facilities as squash and tennis courts, an indoor

The Sheesh Mahal at Amber (above) still glitters brightly with mirrors set into the lime wall of the palace centuries ago. At the City Palace in Jaipur, preference was given to mural art, and in a single courtyard, all the entrances were painted with peacock motifs (facing page).
Following pages: The ramparts of Meherangarh Fort in Jodhpur overlook the Blue City that lies sprawled below; (Pg 44-45) driveway of Rambagh Palace, run as a hotel, in Jaipur, and the Ganesh Pol gateway leading to the palaces within Amber; (Pg 46-47)women gaze at the defensive fortifications of Amber in the distance.

swimming pool and a polo field were added to the palace. When Maharaja Sawai Man Singh II chose it as his principal residence in the 1930s, it was modernised, the suites enlarged, and embellished with elaborate furnishings, among them a Lalique fountain. Raj Mahal is another lovely palace, initially built as the British Residency. Jal Mahal on the road to Amber, was designed as a pleasure pavilion and retreat for duck shooting parties. And, just outside Jaipur, is the palace at Samode, decorated with frescoes in the less formal style that is associated with the Shekhawati area.

Jaipur has a wealth of less famous buildings, each of which has a beauty all its own; wayside temples, garden retreats and picnic pavilions. The entire city was painted pink to celebrate the official visit of the Prince of Wales (later Edward VII), and has remained so ever since, so that it is now referred to as the Pink City , and even a train from New Delhi to Jaipur is called the Pink City Express.

Jodhpur, on the edge of the desert, was once capital of the state of Marwar. Dominating the city is Meherangarh, one of Rajasthan's three great hilltop forts (the other two are Kumbhalgarh and Chittaurgarh). From the fort is a magnificent view of Umaid Bhavan Palace, built of golden sandstone in the middle of the last century. The fort and the palace rise above the surrounding landscape, towering above the city in regal isolation, each on its own hill.

Meherangarh appears impregnable, and with good reason. Its battlements soar four hundred feet above a hill that rises sharply from the surrounding countryside. There is no access to the ramparts, apart from one entrance of seven successive gateways and these are in direct contrast to the delicately lovely residential buildings within. They feature few of the refinements of inlay and wall painting that are evident in states where there was more time for leisure and the pursuit of aesthetics. Nevertheless, Meherangarh has its own architectural drama, such as brilliant stained glass that creates colourful mosaics on the floors with the passage of the sun through the day.

Other fine palaces at Meherangarh include the Moti Mahal, the pearl palace, with its pierced stone screens and the Shringar Chowki where coronation ceremonies were held. Jhanki Mahal in the women's wing has a view of the public areas so that the royal women could watch the day's proceedings. Chandan Mahal was a hall of private audience in which affairs of state were discussed by the luminaries of the state. Rang Mahal is a pleasure palace, the Durbar Takht throne room contains an octagonal *gaddi* upon which the maharaja sat in state. In Meherangarh, the *sheesh mahal* was formerly a house of worship. The palaces in this fort were built in an informal pattern over several centuries. They follow their own rhythm, with narrow staircases serving as the only means of access to the royal residences. The maze of buildings would have made it difficult for any invader to discover the right route to the innermost apartments, and this acted, therefore, as a defense, an essential element since Jodhpur was often at war!

The twentieth century Umaid Bhawan Palace was built in a time of

peace and is open and Western in its design. Maharaja Umaid Singh hired an Englishman, H. V. Lanchester to design his new palace and Lanchester brought with him the heavy civic style of building to which he was accustomed. The building was located on Chhatar Hill and a special rail line was laid to transport building materials to the site. Slowly the great domes rose in royal splendour above the surrounding plain. Its builder and the architect had only one ambition: when complete, it was to rival the Viceroy's Palace in New Delhi, then also under construction.

Under a dome, the like of which no other palace in Rajasthan has, Umaid Bhawan Palace contains over three hundred rooms. It has its own theatre, eight dining rooms, and a banquet hall which seats three hundred people. A Ball Room catered to the Westernised royal lifestyle. Much of the interior of the palace is in the art deco style. In fact it is said to be one of the finest surviving examples of art deco in the world. In the luxurious suites designed for the maharaja and maharani, Indian themes were painted by a visiting Polish artist. Entire baths were carved out of single blocks of marble. Deep within the bowels of the palace is an indoor swimming pool, with a mosaic of zodiac symbols.

The royal family is still in residence in the palace, but so huge is the building that it also houses a magnificent museum and an impressive hotel!

Jaisalmer lies deep in the heart of the desert. It rises out of a sea of sand, its rounded battlements of golden sandstone echoing the colour of the desert sands. A twelfth century settlement, the fort has withstood the ravages of time. Despite its rather remote location, Jaisalmer attracted attention because the early caravan routes passed this way. This in turn gave birth to a rich merchant class that built some of the state's most beautiful *havelis*, or mansions. These handsome buildings are tall by desert standards, and contain a large number of windows screened by panels of intricately carved stone. Their purpose was two-fold: to allow privacy to the women of the house and to catch any hint of breeze and draw it into the inner chambers. Red sandstone from local quarries was used, its thickness acting as a buffer against the heat of the sun. Freshly hewn sandstone was soft, and therefore easily carved, but it hardened with time, providing a perfect building material for the desert.

There are several temples, both Hindu and Jain, outside the fort. The most recent palace built by the royal family also stands outside the fort. Called Badal Mahal, and built a hundred years ago, it is Indo-Saracenic in character. Islamic influence is evident in the fluted pillars, pavilions and the domes; Rajput architecture in the balconies enclosed by stone screens, open courtyards, and the *zenana* with its cool interiors. It is every bit a royal residence, but it pales in comparison to the beautiful *havelis* in the city.

Within the fort is a palace located on the highest point of Tricuta Hill, within a protective wall of double ramparts. Four gateways provided protection to the fort, and several tower-like buildings functioned as lookouts. There are temples within the fort, and there is Jawahar Mahal, another royal residence.

Udaipur is like a fairytale come true. Here, palaces come in dozens, and many of them are romantic residences built on islands in a lake that is the focal point of the city. This profusion of palace architecture is all the more interesting because the house of Mewar, which ruled Udaipur, never accepted Mughal sovereignty. Established in the sixteenth century, the centre of Udaipur was the City Palace, which consists of four major and several minor palaces. It is a fortified complex, for security was in important preoccupation of the early rulers. Part of the complex is the Bada Chowk where the king's infantry and cavalry stood ready for action.

In the City Palace is the Dil Kusha, an early hall of mirrors that also features miniature paintings. A fine mosaic of peacocks characterises Mor Chowk. Bada Mahal is the big garden palace located on a hill within the complex which commands a view over the rest of the palace. Other apartments include Manek Mahal, Khush Mahal, and the opulent Zenana Mahal with its apartments designed for the pomp and ceremony that was part of the royal women's *durbar*. The Durbar Hall is a modern concession to the British Raj. The Jagdish Mandir complex of temples is dedicated to Lord Jagannath, and the temples, especially the central one of the group, are exquisitely carved.

Among Udaipur's other palaces are Sajjan Niwas, Sajjangarh Palace and Sahelion-ki-Bari, but the quintessence of Udaipur is its lake palaces. Located in the middle of Lake Pichola, Jag Niwas, also known as the Lake Palace, is an airy stucco complex complete with dainty balconies, terrace gardens, water fountains, arched windows which frame beautiful views of the lake, and lavishly furnished apartments. These suites were elaborately decorated with paintings, stained glass, and crystal. This palace is now a luxury hotel.

Jag Mandir is a lake retreat built by the maharana for Emperor Shah Jahan. It is made of stone slabs of almost translucent thinness, and it contains spacious courtyards, beautifully proportioned domes, majestic cupolas and apartments whose walls were once inlaid with precious stones. Later additions were made by Maharana Jagat Singh, before he built Jag Niwas as a separate summer palace.

Udaipur was the modern capital of Mewar, but the maharanas originally ruled from their fortified capital at Chittaurgarh. This magnificent city was ransacked so completely that it had to be abandoned. Chittaur is one of the state's finest forts and covers an area of seven hundred acres. Within its fortifications are temples, towers and palaces. Much of Chittaur is in ruins today. It is, however, here that one glimpses the palace of Rani Padmini, the queen who was so beautiful that Allaudin Khilji laid siege on Chittaur to gain her. But Rajput queens are not so easily won, and she committed *jauhar*.

The Chittaur palaces are said to have been beautifully designed and aesthetically decorated, but little remains of their former splendour. However, the two towers inside the ransacked fort, Vijay Stambh and Kirti Stambh are examples of the skilled craftsmanship of the masons who built the fort and remain without parallel in the state.

The mid-fifteenth century Kumbhalgarh Fort, also in Mewar, is a short distance from Chittaurgarh and the last of the three great forts of

Rajasthan. Located on the site of an even earlier fortress, its strategic hilltop location made it practically impregnable. It was however sacked on one occasion in its five hundred years of history. The fort was in itself a complete city with beautiful apartments and lovely palaces. Its crenellated ramparts are built on a rocky peak 3,500 feet high, and its battlements spread over eight miles, enclosing an area that is larger than Chittaurgarh.

Forts and palaces crowd Rajasthan; even the smallest of settlements has a building of rare and great beauty. But no mention of the state's architecture would be complete without reference to the beautiful Jain temples that flourished in almost every principality.

Not least among these is the complex of Jain temples at Ranakpur. The central temple in the complex is called Chaumukha and is an interesting example of the richness of carving and sculptural art in medieval Rajasthan. The temple covers an area of 40,000 square feet, has 29 halls and contains 1,444 pillars; no one pillar is like another in the detail and wealth of the delicate carvings that adorn all of them.

Mount Abu, Rajasthan's only hill resort, where the maharajas built summer palaces, is also known for its large number of Jain temples. The Dilwara Jain temple complex contains a wealth of beautifully proportioned and richly carved temples set amidst a mango grove.

If Rajasthan is a repository of the finest palaces in the country, it also provides evidence of the lifestyles that governed their building. They were largely martial fortifications inside which the inherent sensitivity of the Rajput kings led to the creation of palaces that blended the necessities of state administration, defence and the pursuits of leisure with graceful elegance. Golden Rajasthan has no greater wealth than these buildings from the past.

The Mubarak Mahal courtyard of the City Palace in Jaipur (below) is open to visitors, as is the entrance courtyard of Amber Fort (facing page, below), but the Jal Mahal (facing page, above), once a hunting lodge, though visible from the roadside, is restricted for guests. Jaipur is close to Delhi, and acts as an entry point for an exploration of Rajasthan.

CRAFTS
and Celebration

Camels are often prettily decorated (above), especially during festivals, and there are even songs that have been composed about the braids and beads they wear on such occasions.
Facing page: Tazias make their way down a Jaipur street on the occasion of Muharram. The Hawa Mahal was especially built to allow the women of the royal household to look out on to such celebrations without themselves being seen by the people on the street.

IN RAJASTHAN, VIVID TONES OF RED, PINK, blue, saffron and green are made even more brilliant by the addition of gilt and silver borders, mirrors, sequins and printed motifs. They add gaiety and an air of festivity to the smallest village fair. In an area which is still largely rural, fairs and festivals provide a joyous opportunity to meet friends and relatives and to transact business in an atmosphere of cheerful good humour. Handicrafts come into their own at such times, for each area has its own special crafts. Beautifully made objects of everyday use are a part of every Rajasthani's life. Plain fabrics are brightened with coloured tie-and-dye, diagonal *leheriya* stripes and a range of block pints. Factory-made shoes are redundant, for few can give you the fit, the delicate embroidery and the resilient strength of the hand-made Rajasthani *jooti*. Homes, even the humblest mud hut, are decorated; patchwork *torans* adorn doorways; food is cooked in vessels of burnished copper. Mirrors, broken glass bangles, fragments of fabric and pottery are all used to beautify the home and even mud becomes a decorative material from which relief can be moulded.

Women who dress traditionally, wear a *lehenga*, an ankle length skirt, with a *kurti-kanchli*, two garments that become a blouse, completed with *odhni* or mantle. An essential part of the dress of every woman is heavy jewellery, a *rakhri* on the forehead, wrists covered with *chura* or ivory bangles, and *paijeb* or substantial anklets. The nobility and educated upper classes now usually wear *saris*. This is almost always a chiffon, and worn in a particularly elegant style, but come a marriage, and the women are off to Jodhpur to pick the bride her trousseau, for this is the centre for the marvellously beautiful gold *zardozi* embroidery. Bridal footwear for the bride and her groom will invariably come from Jaipur; certainly their jewellery will. For yes, even the groom must wear sufficient jewellery, probably a seven string necklace of pearls embellished with emeralds and rubies down his brocade tunic, buttons of gold to enrich his white *bund-gala*, and a gold *kalgi* or pin to set in his turban.

Jaipur is one of very few centres in the world where gemstones are still cut and polished by hand. Buyers from round the world come here to place their orders with gemologists who have practised their trade for generations.

And the world's most beautiful jewels are set in gold and exported around the world. Entire streets of jewellers practise the art; and strings of semi-precious stones are sold literally for a song.

Mina or enamel-work jewellery has given rise to a popular sub-art, that of enamelling on silver, and on other metals, with designs filled with glowing colours. Miniature silver elephants worked in enamel and bejewelled, make extraordinary objets d'art, and when the skill of these craftsmen is used on copper the result is beautiful table tops, wall plaques and a wonderful range of bowls. They also sculpt delicate figures in onyx, jade, smoky topaz, and other gemstones.

Some of the intricacy of this work is reflected in their statuary too. The marble mines of Makrana surround Jaipur, and these mines supplied the marble with which the Taj Mahal in Agra was built. Marble is quarried now with the help of expensive Italian machines, and shaped as tiles, or as blocks supplied to artisans to practise their trade. The result is a rich variety of statues, mostly religious in character, that are supplied to Indian temples. But smaller statues, pedestals, urns, bowls, table tops, planters, vases, and ashtrays are also fashioned in Jaipur's many workshops.

In a sense, all that is available in Jaipur is also available elsewhere, but Jaipur remains the centre of many of the state's flourishing arts. Among these are blue pottery, a Persian art that was introduced into the country by the Muslims. Over the years it lost royal patronage and was almost obliterated till it was re-introduced by a potter who also makes some of the loveliest miniatures in the country. Kripal Singh Shekhawat runs his studio in a desultory fashion. His living room and his garden contain shelves full of glowing pots bearing his signature, waiting to be shipped to all parts of the world. His wife is unhappy that the studio cannot accommodate all that he produces, but the couple are overjoyed at the renewed popularity of blue pottery. In a sense blue pottery is a misnomer, for it is made of crushed quartz, fuller's earth and sodium sulphate. The pots are moulded, only their lips shaped on a simple potter's wheel. The surface is painted in characteristic motifs, using copper sulphate for the lighter blue and copper oxide for the deeper, royal blue. The popularity of the art has now ensured the survival of several studios, and Kripal Singh Shekhawat has turned his attention to other colours (green and yellow, and even pink), and to motifs that range from figures inspired by the Ajanta and Ellora caves to Chinese and Japanese art forms!

Rajasthan has its share of stone cutters and sculptors, but nowhere do they reach the excellence of the Barmer craftsmen who chisel red sandstone into works of poetry. So richly is the stone chiselled and picked out, it resembles lace.

In nearby Bikaner, where the finest carpets were once made, the craft is still practised in the city's prison. In fact, these beautiful carpets, almost all of them being exported, are known as jail-carpets! But a craft that is characteristic of this desert city is that of painting in gold leaf on camel skin. The inner hide of the camel is buffed and moulded into basic shapes for lampshades, vases, containers for expensive perfumes and decorative frames. This is then painted

A 'kachi ghodi' dance (above), one of several entertainments offered in the state, and (facing page) people gathered to attend fairs, an occasion they use for social interaction as well as for transactions of commerce. Following pages: Views from the camel fair at Pushkar, an event with a history so hoary, no one can recall when it first began. But for hundreds of years, people have gathered here on the occasion of the full moon of Kartika-Poornima (November), and little has changed in recent years but for the presence of a handful of tourists who come to participate in the fair.

with delicately gilded gesso work floral motifs.

Carpets are also made in Jaipur, of wool, while the *dhurrie* or cotton rug industry was practically launched from here. A new and fashionable demand is for antiques, and this had given rise to manufacturers who create objects and furniture in the fashion of earlier decades, and impart 'age' through a variety of processes including acid washing, immersing in cauldrons of boiling water, and applying various dyes. These are seldom sold as antiques, only as look-alikes, and therefore meet the urban demand in ingenious Rajasthani fashion. Major centres for these arts are Jaipur and Jodhpur. Udaipur is known for its inlay furniture.

Sanganer, a village near Jaipur, is famed for its hand-block printed fabric, in geometric and floral patterns, and for its hand-made paper. In Bagru, hand-block prints are made in more earthy colours, usually browns and black, with startling geometric designs.

Rajasthan is also known for its paintings, both miniatures in the Mughal style, and folk paintings on fabric and paper. Some of the art has been reduced to street level, so popular has it become, and the quality consequently varies a great deal. There are, however, artists who still maintain the standards for earlier, more beautiful craftsmanship. The *pichwais* of Rajasthan are sold all over, the *phads* less so. *Pichwais* are painted on black fabric and usually depict stories from the life of Lord Krishna, *phads* tell of folk heroes in bright colours, usually on a white background. At one time, Rajasthani paintings were painted directly on to the walls of homes, and each region had its style, in which the human figures are characterised by elongated noses and stylised eyebrows. Those of Udaipur were filled with a wealth of detail, and many depicted court life. Kota featured elephants in a characteristic green colour. Bikaner came to be known for its paintings of horses. Kota, because of its location perhaps, depicted a large number of hunting scenes.

As in art and craft, festivals are an intrinsic part of life. The *bhopas* and the *dholis*, all itinerant musicians, are usually men, and they use simple instruments such as the harmonium and the *tabla*, to accompany their songs. Their full-bodies voices carry easily across the silent desert spaces.

Forms of dance and music that originated in Rajasthan were usually folk celebrations. The only classical form that traces its origins and growth to Rajasthan is *kathak* from the Jaipur *gharana*. Among the most popular dance forms is the *ghoomar*, usually a private performance by women of the home, in the inner courtyards of the house on a festive occasion, usually a marriage. Traditionally, men of the house were denied access to the performance, though now of course it is performed almost everywhere. Women in their brilliant Rajasthani skirts swirl around an imaginary circle, in clockwise and anti-clockwise movement. The dance steps and hand movements are fairly simple, but there is a rhythmic flow to the pattern of the dance that is particularly pleasing.

The *kachchi ghodi* dance on the other hand is performed almost exclusively by men, the spectacle is one of a bridegroom's party locked in battle, and there is much brandishing of swords and riding of horses in the tradition

of the puppeteers. Rajasthan's puppeteers are artisans par excellence, controlling with their fingers the movements of a number of puppets, while singing or conversing in shrill tones to the beat of a *morchang* or jew's harp. Another men's dance is the *gair*, in which men move in a circle keeping time with long sticks in their hands with which they strike those held by other dancers to a rhythmic clacking beat.

One of the most mesmerising performances is the *sapera* dance performed by members of the snake charmers' community. The dance is fast, and the flowing colours of the dancers' skirts lend it an unusual tonal quality. The *charee* dance is performed by women with brass vessels on their head, dressed to welcome a bridegroom. The vessels contains smouldering cotton seeds.

In Bikaner, dancers perform a death-defying fire dance when they prance on a bed of live, hot coals, all the more spectacular when performed on a dark night, with the coals flaming a brilliant red. Almost as daring is the *bhavai* dance where performers balance seven or nine pitchers on their heads while dancing bare feet on the edges of swords, or on bits of broken glass!

During the *terah tali* dance, performers sit in front of an image of the deity Ramdeoji, and perform intricate movements to the pulse of thirteen cymbals. Some unusual instruments used by musicians in the desert include the *bankia* or trumpet, the jew's harp, the *algoza* or twin harps with their high cadence, the *ektara*, or one-stringed instrument, and the *matka* or pitcher which is used as a percussion instrument.

Festivals almost exclusively for women include Gangaur and Teej, the latter associated with the monsoon. Women dress in *leheriya* striped garments, and spend the day decorating swings with flowers on which they sit with their spouses. During both festivals prayers are offered before images of Parvati and Shiva, and the festivals celebrate love, matrimony

Below: Baneshwar Fair
Facing page: A tribal woman is fully decked up as she mans a stall of embroidered textiles at a local fair.
Following pages: A woman decorates her modest home with 'mandana' or drawings of rice flour; a potter adds finishing touches to a statue of a folk hero; (Pg 64-65) frescoes such as this embellish the walls of palaces and havelis of Shekhawati.

and conjugal bless. Gifts are exchanged between women of the house, and street processions led by images of the god and goddess weave through the streets of cities and villages.

Rajasthan's other major festival is Dussehra, celebrated as a nine day period of fasting, with people partaking of only one meal in a day. For most communities, this also means a vegetarian diet; the Rajputs, however, pay obeisance before the Devi by sacrificing a goat before the goddess of power, and eating the mutton as the food blessed by the god, *prasad*! In Bikaner, Holi, the festival of colour in honour of Lord Krishna, is a ten-day event and involves spontaneous community singing and dancing. Yet another religious festival is the Baneshwar Fair held in Dungarpur near Udaipur. This large tribal fair draws people from all over the state as well as from neighbouring Gujarat and Madhya Pradesh. Held at the confluence of the rivers Mahi and Som, prayers are said to Lord Shiva, and devotees take a ritual dip in the river.

Major Rajasthani celebrations are necessarily socio-economic in character and include the popular cattle fair at Pushkar. Over the years, Pushkar has become Rajasthan's most famous fair. Prayers are said to Lord Brahma, but the business at hand is trading, for camels, horses and even cattle for foodstuff and condiments, and the crafts of the desert. It is a delightful experience, full of colour and joy. Unlike Pushkar is the cattle fair at Nagpur held in January-February, which is an all male affair. The men wear white *kurtas* and *dhotis*, and colourful turbans, and there is brisk trading here, for it is the country's largest cattle fair and there is little time, therefore, for the pleasures of singing and dancing. A similar fair is held near Bikaner, at Kolayat, around the same time as Pushkar. These and myriad small village fairs provide opportunities for meeting and for matchmaking. Yet another livestock fair is held at Jhalraptan. The Chandrabhaga fair is interesting for it provides a glimpse into the life and rhythm of the Hadoti people.

Since the celebrations of Rajasthan are so colourful and since many of them, other than the fairs, are private celebrations, the tourism department in Rajasthan has decided to re-create these celebrations for visitors. These include the Desert Festival in Jaisalmer, Brij Festival held around Holi in Bharatpur, the Elephant Festival at around the same time in Jaipur, and the Marwar Festival in Jodhpur. Though these are organised affairs, one can be sure they will carry with them the romance of golden Rajasthan. Colour, celebration, rhythm, the deep resonance of a musical voice...

But for the people no celebration would be complete without obeisance before their *kul-devis* and *devatas*, community gods and goddesses. Every princely state in Rajasthan has these deities where the first family offered prayers. These gods still have their abodes, and they still have their devotees. So much so that in Bikaner, at Deshnoke, the tutelar deity is Karni Mata, and the temple provides sanctuary to rats. But then this temple of the rats should be no contradiction. In Rajasthan, the unusual soon becomes acceptable. For the heart of this colourful land with its chivalrous men, beautiful women, creative arts and opulent palaces is a desert. No wonder then that golden Rajasthan is a land of glorious contradictions.

Rituals and
CUSTOMS

Women are major participants in most social and religious events, whether it is peddling their wares at a village fair (above) or offering prayers to a tree (facing page), arguably one of the desert's rare resources.

WHEN THEY WERE IN POWER, the princes of Rajasthan often ruled wisely and well and if a system of eleborate rituals and customs governed their lives, there were often good reasons for them. It was political strategy that dictated who should anoint a new king, or why the ladies of the *zenana* should be kept in *purdah*.

When the princes signed treaties with the increasingly powerful British rulers of India, their power became a mockery. They were often admonished as children are by the British authorities, and their position as rulers was reduced to an empty show. They tried to appease their new overlords with lavish entertainment such as shoots that were cleverly arranged to give their guests an advantage that helped even novitiate hunters bag magnificent game, the like of which they had never seen. What remained to the princes was money; so much, in fact, that they did not quite know what to do with it. Very often, therefore, they sailed off to London, to spend it on hundreds of Savile Row suits, Cartier jewels and fleets of Rolls Royces.

Divested of power, idle and rich, many of them became eccentric. Others, vitiated by the hate that congealed in their bosoms as they despaired at themselves for not having the strength to defend their authority against the British, turned to alcohol and opium. They lived out their lives in the confines of their palaces, far removed from the realities of life.

There were those, however, who continued to work with dedication, devoting their energies and resources to the welfare of their people. Amongst them were the first feminist princesses who fought against the *purdah* and went on to pioneer social and educational work in their states.

Many royal families adopted a more Western lifestyle. Their royal garments of silk and brocade were replaced by fashionable linen suits. The royal women shed their saris for slacks. Indian food was replaced by Western cuisine and palace cooks who could not properly pronounce what they were cooking mastered the art of making French onion soup and roast, pies and exotic pastries.

Yet all the while, in the traditional rituals of their lives, the royal families clung to their beliefs and customs. Some, perhaps, were afraid of being thought superstitious by their Western friends. Nevertheless they continued to abide by them, so deeply embedded were these beliefs in their lives and their minds.

The birth of a new prince was accompanied by ceremonial patterns established in the past. Doctors were summoned to attend to the pregnant princesses, but when the labour pains began, they were banished outside, and a string tied to the foot of the princess in labour. The end of the string was held by the state astrologer to whom the exact moment of the birth was signalled so that the child's horoscope could be accurately charted. Despite their Western education the princes of Rajasthan continued to marry early, often had several wives despite their Western sophistication and their advanced "modern" views. There were ceremonial coronation ceremonies when they ascended thrones that were no longer truly theirs. They bestowed gifts on festive occasions, often after taking permission from the British. They dressed in traditional splendour when the occasion demanded, but sought fashionable Western attire for their daily lives.

It was a schizophrenic lifestyle that worked after a fashion. Independence gave the princes of Rajasthan their last illusion of power, for each one was asked to choose whether his state would join India or Pakistan, but even as they were making up their minds, the authorities had already decided their fate.

The illusion continued for a few more years, until the government clamped down on their privy purses and the royal lifestyle of Rajasthan was consigned to history.

Yet, was it? Visit a royal home today, even the humblest – for all of them did not prosper in the mainstream of life – and you will be extended royal courtesies. A deep bow, visitors who still do not look into the eyes of their erstwhile rulers, liveried servants, white glove tea service... and certain royals who will not ever take the name of former renegade states, but will willingly spell them out for you! On festivals some may still be weighed against coins. And if you are a friend, you may still be welcomed with a palmful of opium – enough to knock you out for a few days if you are not in the habit of this particular indulgence!

Stories abound on the ceremonial usage of opium in the courts of Rajasthan. In its current and somewhat limited form it is used as a form of greeting close friends on festive or ritual occasions. But it was not always so.

The use of opium is so ancient that there is no clear indication of when it first entered court life and became entrenched there. In the desert, it was used as a panacea against illness, to dress battle wounds and as a soporific to the aged and children in times of sickness. It is quite possible that opium came into royal use to ease the fatigue and wounds of battle. From there into the palace was but a short journey. Evidently, at some stage it became a matter of prestige to serve this drug and before long it was being used to welcome guests. However, it was in Jodhpur that the ritual of serving opium became a formal art. Other states and *thikanas*, the homes of nobles called thakurs, served it too, but the ceremony is associated with

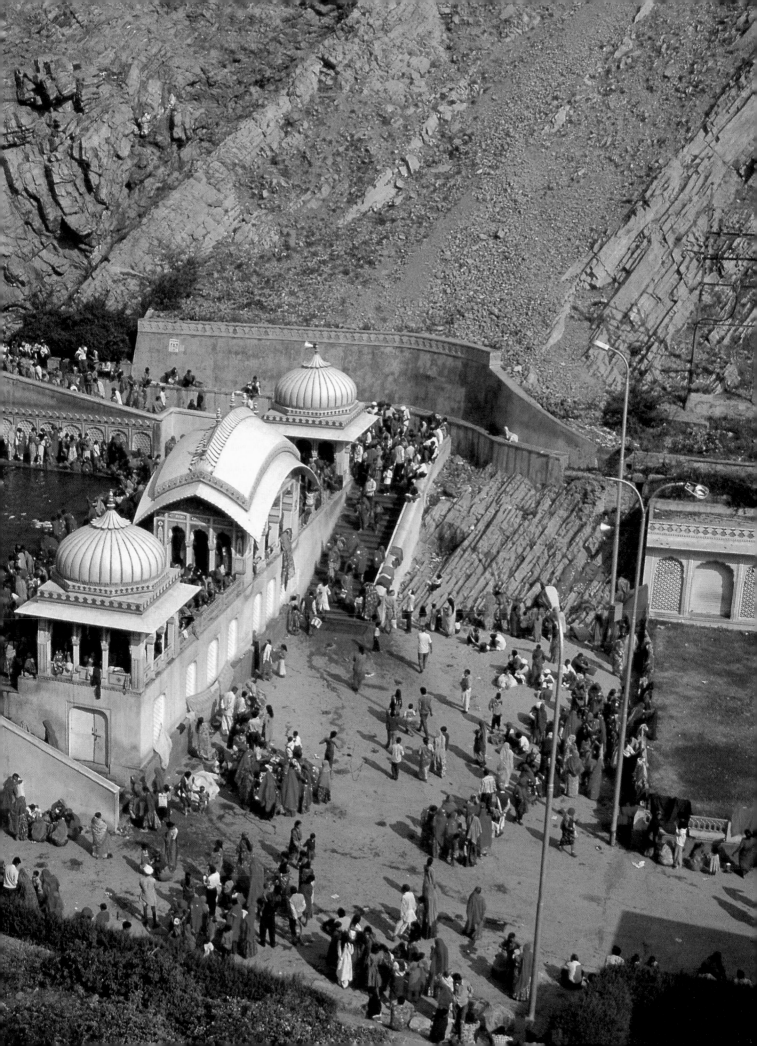

Jodhpur, and perhaps with good reason for even though it is now illegal, opium is still offered to visitors in greeting in any village of the Bishnoi community who are settled around Jodhpur.

Opium began to be served when a king wished to express his happiness, or when he wished to remove a person from his path without a royal decree. An incident is recounted of Jaipur's Ishwari Singh poisoning his minister, Dewan Keshav Das Khatri with an overdose of opium. Ishwari Singh, the eldest son of Sawai Jai Singh II, was the accepted heir to the throne of Jaipur. However, he knew he would not succeed without conflict because the throne had been promised to any male heir born to Jai Singh's second consort, the princess of Udaipur. Jai Singh himself was alive to the political implications of the situation, and it is said he would have had his own second son, Madho Singh, killed rather than have internecine struggles over the throne. Fortunately, a soldier helped Madho Singh to flee to Udaipur, thereby defusing the tension. When news reached Ishwari Singh that the minister Keshav Das wanted to aid Madho Singh's return to Jaipur, he poisoned the conspirator with opium.

It is said that one maharaja ordered his courtiers, who were serving opium, to give his eldest paternal uncle *dooni*, twice as much. When the revels were over, he found that his decree had been interpreted by his courtiers as the grant of a village named Dooni to his uncle!

It is strange that though the women of the *zenana* did not shy away from alcohol, opium was more or less shunned. Eccentricities were not always opium-induced, and tales of strange incidents have been passed down the generations. On one occasion the famed poet, Surajmal, went to the state of Sirohi to visit a princess from Bundi who had married the king of the state. There, the queen, who had just received a new *poshak*, dress, had it sent to the poet seeking his approval. Sarcastically he told the maid who carried the lovely garments: "Yes, indeed, it is very nice! Ask her, will she wear this *poshak* when she commits *sati?*"

And as it happened, it was in those very clothes that the princess consigned herself to the flames!

Sati is a sensitive issue today, but it was not always so. Once it was considered an honour to immolate oneself on the flames of one's husband's funeral pyre. There are stories of princesses willingly consigning themselves to the flames at the death of their husband but usually it was *jauhar* that took place — mass immolations in case of defeat in war to save oneself dishonour at the hands of the enemy.

When princes went to war, they arranged a signal so that the women, in the event of defeat, would do the honourable deed of committing *jauhar* rather than face the humiliation of life in an enemy court. The system was not flawless, and once when the signal of defeat was raised by mistake, a victorious king came back to find only the ashes of his queens.

It was not always out of love for their husbands that the queens committed *sati*, however. From childhood, it was impressed upon them

that *jauhar* and *sati* were honourable. For those who lived, life as a widow was probably intolerable. At times when a hasty decision had to be taken, often *jauhar* seemed the easy way out. With the weight of custom and tradition upon them, and in an atmosphere in which honour was valued above life, there often seemed no alternative. In another form, *sati* was also used to spur the princes to war. There is a popular ballad about a Hada queen, newly married and still to consummate her marriage, whose husband was reluctantly called to war. The infatuated young prince could not concentrate on the battle and asked a courtier to go back home and ask his queen for a token of her love. The queen saw the peril that lay ahead for the kingdom, and it is said she had her head sent to the prince in the hope that it would keep his mind from straying from battle!

Today, if you visit any fort in Rajasthan, you will see the poignant handprints of the queens who committed *jauhar* by the entrance gates.

The birth of a son meant the proclamation that an heir had been born to the royal home, naturally a moment of celebration. It was such an important event that the mother was given the privilege of wearing colours reserved specially for mothers of male children. At the birth of a male child, *thalis*, silver platters, were used as gongs to announce to the world that an heir had been born. Jaggery or unrefined sugar, was distributed all over the kingdom to broadcase news of this important event.

When the first male child was born to a family, the child's maternal uncle presented the new mother with a *peeliya poshak*; a set of yellow garments, decorated with red motifs. Other gifts of new clothes were in the same colour. A women who wear the *peeliya* stands proud in any Rajput home even today.

Colours in fact, play an important role in the homes of Rajasthan. No bride, no married woman, in fact, from a Rajput family will wear black; yet strangely on the festive occasion of Diwali, in Jaipur, this colour of the night is worn embellished with the glitter of gold that blazes on black in a manner that is symbolic of this festival of lights and fireworks. Blue and light green are considered colours of mourning, worn by widows and taboo for a new bride, though these may be worn with the addition of *zardozi* embroidery and brocade work. The one colour that remains out-of-bounds most is the colour that suggests widowhood all over the desert and has a haunting quality of finality: brown. It would appear that women dress to bring cheer to the arid dessert, to defy its monotonous dun sand. Theirs is a world awash with bright colours, and often the formal dress of the men (white and black are favourite colours) complements the vibrant colours worn by the women. Not only are the fabrics gaily coloured, their effect is all the more dramatic because of the motifs used upon them: a range of block printed patterns, vivid tie-dyes, and monsoon *leheriyas* or stripes with their rain-washed effect. It is perhaps little wonder then that the colour that is considered Rajasthan's dearest is red and according to a popular saying there are three gems in the desert: a *dhola* (lover), a *marian* (beloved), and red, the colour of love.

In the palaces of Rajasthan, ritual became such an important part of daily life that the royal house of Jaipur had a book on ceremonial procedure printed with details of what to wear, and the order in which nobles and courtiers would proceed during ceremonies held at birthdays, deaths, accessions to the throne, visits by heads of state, festivals and fairs and so on.

Style and fashion have played a major role in the evolution of the Rajput turban, known as the *safa* .The earliest record of turbans in India shows that they were white, and tied *potoli* or bag fashion. The current fashion of the safa dates back to pre-Mughal times, for the Mughals brought with them thicker turbans, and embellished them with jewellery. This eventually led to the birth of the '*atpati*' safa formed when the Rajput turban was adapted by Mughal Emperor Akbar for his court. Later, Emperor Jehangir modified the style a little, and soon the elaborate court *safa* was adopted by the courtiers. With the weakening of Mughal power, independent *rajas* started their own style of tying a *safa*, and eventually these differed not only between different states, but between different groups in the same state. The currently popular manner of tying the *safa* has been adapted from the Marathi turban. The tie-and-dye safa has come to be known as the Jodhpuri safa, and to this kingdom also goes the credit for introducing the Jodhpur breeches adopted by polo players the world over and the '*band-gala*' or 'closed –neck' coats, which are frequently worn by government officials in India today.

A Rajput cannot now wear a white *safa* if his father is alive, and so white *safas* have become the customary colour of mourning. During weddings, the most widely used colours are saffron and red.

The *tilak*, the royal ceremony of accession to the throne, was an important ritual, and one that was kneely contested, for though succession was hereditary, it frequently involved political machinations and intrigue. The role of the British in Delhi, who sought a pliable ruler, the internal strifes of the state, and the rare amity between brothers made the appointment of the heir a very delicate issue. If the princes were to have had their way, more than one of them would have been crowned king. But the *tilak* ceremony itself was a safeguard against such an event.

The *tilak* is a mark of victory, and it is, therefore, not surprising, that in Udaipur the auspicious red mark on the forehead was made not by powdered colour, but by blood. In the case of Bikaner, only a member of the community known as Godera Jats could place this mark on the forehead of the king, for it was on their territory that the founder of the state had laid his capital, and he had bestowed upon them the honour of placing the *tilak* on the king's forehead for all time. The same honour in Jaipur was reserved for member of the Brahmin caste.

What was more elaborate, however, was the ceremony of *nazar* or the paying of tribute. Held as a formal *durbar* at the court, attendance was strictly ordered by rank. Besides visiting heads of state and nobles, *nazar* was also offered by heads of different communities and craft-guilds. The amount to be paid as tribute was specified in advance, and the gold and silver coins were to enrich the state's treasury.

No war was fought, no major task undertaken without the ruler and the royal household worshipping at the family shrine. Maharajas walked barefoot to these shrines before long journeys, to seek the blessings of the family deity. Interestingly, one of the things forbidden to Rajput rulers were journeys overseas because it was believed that one would lose one's caste by so doing. However, only a few years after the British established their hegemony, journeying to the Continent became a favourite princely pastime. Nevertheless, certain eccentricities persisted. While they would drink wine in the bars of Chelsea, they would dine only at their temporary residences where their own cooks prepared elaborate meals in the manner of home. The first maharaja of Jaipur to journey to England had three huge silver vessels made so that he could carry drinking water with him from India. The two surviving containers may be seen at the City Palace museum in Jaipur even today.

The pomp of Rajasthan's royal past has still not disappeared entirely. In a modern democracy, the people remain loyal to members of former royal families. When there is strife, they still go to their erstwhile rulers for advice and material help. Little of the latter is forthcoming, for though some may still be wealthy their power belongs to yesterday. Many of them have moved with the times and are now industrialists, hoteliers and member of the Indian parliament...

The grandeur of palaces and mansions remains in Rajasthan, but people now stroll casually through them; several are government offices; and inevitably they are surrounded by pedestrian examples of modern architecture at its most unimaginative. Cars, rickshaws, and bicycles clutter streets where royal processions once moved at a stately pace through the length of the day.

The birth of a male child continues to be a cause for rejoicing even today, for land is passed on to a male heir. Marriages are still arranged between families. Widows no longer commit *sati* but they still do not remarry. Weddings continue to be occasions for opulent extravagances. The wedding of a modern Rajput city executive is likely to be an elaborate affair, as his ancestor's was. The bride will wear a traditional skirt and jewellery and the groom will be dressed in a brocade tunic and turban and will carry a sword. They will bow in deep obeisance, wish *Khamaghani*, and then converse with each other in perfect, unaccented English. This is not a contradiction.

The roots of Rajput society go back thousands of years. Despite an adaptation to contemporary lifestyles, it is not so easy to turn one's back on one's roots.

Caparisoned elephants during a celebration in Jaipur (facing page, above). The elephant was a symbol of royalty, and formed an essential flank that led charges during battles. Today, it is more likely to be depicted in works of art and architecture. It is more usual for people to use the camel for transportation, while families prefer to travel in cattle-drawn carts (facing page, below). Preceding page: Women make offerings to ancient stone deities (above) while henna is used to decorate the palm on all special occasions, and particularly for weddings. Pages 74-75: People gather on the banks of Pushkar Lake for a holy dip on the Kartik Poornima.

For many, the day begins with an offering of
prayers to the sun god, following a holy dip
in a pond or lake close to a temple. The
Rajasthanis are a devout people, and have an
abiding faith in the divine.